Greenhouse Gardening! Discover And Quickly Learn How To Use Greenhouse's To Grow Vegetables And Do It Organically!

Copyright 2018

Disclaimer

This book is not intended as a substitute for the medical advice of physicians. The reader should regularly consult a physician in matters relating to his/her health and particularly with respect to any symptoms that may require diagnosis or medical attention.

Although the author and publisher have made every effort to ensure that the information in this book was correct at press time, the author and publisher do not assume and hereby disclaim any liability to any party for any loss, damage, or disruption caused by errors or omissions, whether such errors or omissions result from negligence, accident, or any other cause.

This document is geared towards providing exact and reliable information in regards to the topic and issue covered. The publication is sold with the idea that the publisher is not required to render accounting, officially permitted, or otherwise, qualified services. If advice is necessary, legal or professional, a practiced individual in the profession should be ordered.

- From a Declaration of Principles which was accepted and approved equally by a Committee of the American Bar Association and a Committee of Publishers and Associations.

In no way is it legal to reproduce, duplicate, or transmit any part of this document in either electronic means or in printed format. Recording of this publication is strictly prohibited and any storage of this document is not allowed unless with written permission from the publisher. All rights reserved.

The information provided herein is stated to be truthful and consistent, in that any liability, in terms of inattention or otherwise, by any usage or abuse of any policies, processes, or directions contained within is the solitary and utter responsibility of the recipient reader. Under no circumstances will any legal responsibility or blame be held against the publisher for any reparation, damages, or monetary loss due to the information herein, either directly or indirectly.

Respective authors own all copyrights not held by the publisher.

The information herein is offered for informational purposes solely, and is universal as so. The presentation of the information is without contract or any type of guarantee assurance.

The trademarks that are used are without any consent, and the publication of the trademark is without permission or backing by the trademark owner. All trademarks and brands within this book are for clarifying purposes only and are the owned by the owners themselves, not affiliated with this document.

Introduction

Greenhouse gardening is a ton of fun, and you can definitely grow some awesome stuff Think about it, you have a place where plants can grow during all seasons, and you can have crops all year round.

It's also a great way to help start seeds early on before you transplant them over to the ground, which in turn will allow for more plants to grow, and a better crop yield.

But, how do you do it? What do you need to begin? What are some of the best ways to control the environment that you're about to create? Well, you're about to find out.

This book will give you a comprehensive look at everything that you need to begin greenhouse gardening. It's simple really, and often, it's definitely something that does take a bit of time to get started with, and might be a bit pricy, but you'll be able to net some great, really tasty, and healthy foods from it. Plus, you'll have way more plants than ever before, which is totally fun, and worth everything that you do for this. So what are you waiting for? It's time to get started.

Chapter 1: What you Need to Begin

The first question you will ask yourself, is what you need to begin to start this. We obviously need a greenhouse, but what else? Well, you're about to find out. Having all of this on hand will make your greenhouse gardening easier, and while you might not know what kinds of plants you want just yet, knowing a few of the different things that you need before you begin will definitely help you.

Freestanding or Attached?

First thing you need to consider, is whether or not you're going to go the freestanding route, or the attached route. Both of these have their pros and cons, and it's important to weight each of the options when choosing a greenhouse for yourself.

Freestanding means that it doesn't have an attachment to a house or structure. These are the typical glass greenhouses that you see in pictures and such. These are usually made of glass because they conduct the heat and light way easier than other such materials, but it can be a bit pricy. There are other options too, which we will go over later. This gives you a lot more light, so if you're in an area where your house gets bad light, it might be best to go the freestanding route. The biggest disadvantage, is more labor and pricier since you got to build that fourth side.

In contrast, the attached means that it is attached to a home or a structure. This is good if you're not totally sure you want a full greenhouse, or you just don't want to go all the way to the middle of your backyard during the winter to take care of plants. This is built on three different sides, attached to the house or structure. It has the advantage of less building, can be closer, and might be easier, but the major disadvantage if only three sides, which does limit the light. When you're building this, do assess where your home gets the most light before you begin building your greenhouse, so that you know whether or not you're going the freestanding route, or the attached route when it comes to building.

Soil to grow

Next you need the soil. Soil is super important, since it is what you'll be using to grow these plants. You need to make sure that the soil isn't unsterilized, because that actually has parasites in it, and it might cause you major issues in the long term because of this. unsterilized soil is a lot cheaper, yes, but it actually can affect the overall growth of your greenhouse if you're not careful. If you're going to take soil from your backyard, sterilize it so that it doesn't have parasites. You can bake it at 250 degrees to help get rid of the parasites in there. You can then mix it with fertilizer and then blend it together, and while it might be fun to do this, sometimes it might be better to just splurge on soil. Soil is a huge part, because this is where the plants will grow, and if a blight or any sort of parasite gets into this, it often does mean curtains for your greenhouse gardening adventures.

Light

Light is a huge part of your greenhouse gardening. Chances are, you're doing a chunk of this growing during the winter, where the light is often lessened. Getting growing bulbs, or even just some heating lamps, in order to help get these little plants started can make a huge difference.

If you don't have enough light, it can be quite hard for them to germinate, and in turn, you might end up being too late on growing this. When it comes to growing, you should try to do a lot of it early on, and begin it at the get-go so that you're not spending extra time during the prime growing months. These little growing bulbs can be a good way to make sure that the plants get what they need.

On the flip side, some plants don't need to have light on them all the time. Maybe you've got plants that do, and plants that don't. In that case, get one of those little shade cloths and throw it over this, making sure that they're not affected too much by the light, or lack thereof. Basically, just use each of these to help with ensuring that the plants get the right amount of light.

Seeds of plants to start

You've got two options for how you want to grow, either seeds, or starters. Seeds are much cheaper, and often you get a lot more for what you're paying for. Starters are plants that are already started, and might be the best option if you end up starting late. They are more expensive, but they often require less patience, and on the flip side, seeds are way cheaper, but they take much longer to grow, and it might create worry if you don't see results right away. Both can be bought at a nursery, or even a home improvement store.

When you do this, make sure that you have plants that are sturdy, able to withstand and have protection against elements, and don't have disease or pests. This is a huge part, and its why people try to go to the local nursery, since there is less of a chance for aphids to go on there, and you should make sure that you're getting them from a reliable source.

Fertilizer

Fertilizer is something that will help the plant grow. It's essentially plant food, but often, like anything else, you could end up giving it too much, and if that happens, it could end up being bad. You should also take a look at the soil that you have, and if you have soil you bought, you should check to see if it's already fortified with nutrients. They're usually in there, and enough to keep the plant healthy for a little bit.

You should put fertilizer in there with a diluted mixture of it to help get the plants used to it, and from there continue to feed it a little bit more and more. don't give it too much, too fast. Doing so is how many times the pH balance of the roots changes, and it will make the plant acidic, and that in turn can damage the roots, causing the plant to suffer as well. So, be smart, follow direction, and take it nice and slow.

Potters

Next are the potters, which are the containers used to house the plants. Everything in this case should be made sterilized, and you should make sure that if you do have a planter, don't be afraid to go big if it needs it, but within reason. You should make sure that the planter is deep enough so that the roots can be sturdy, and it has room for this. If you have the roots bound to the bottom, it actually can make it unhealthy for them.

You should sterilize before you throw a plant in there, simply because there are parasites in some of the soil that you get from the backyard, and you don't know where it's been. You should do half water and half vinegar, and then start to remove the debris here and then rinse with some water before you put the soil and plants in there. This is usually what you have to do if you're going to be reusing a planter.

Glazing

One thing you have to do before you begin as well, is glaze the greenhouse. Once you build it, you should make sure that the sunlight comes in, without the elements attached. Think about it, if it's the dead of winter, it might be super warm in terms of the sunlight, but if you don't glaze it, you're actually going to let in bitter-cold temperatures, and if you do that, that's how you kill plants. You should cover it in polycarbonate and make sure that you have it rightfully set up so that the light gets transmitted.

It's encouraged to have someone build this for you, but you can build it yourself if you so desire, it just takes less work, but it can be cheaper as well.

Choosing a site

Finally, let's talk about the site. You should make sure that you think long and hard before you put the site in, since the closer it is to your home, the chances are that you'll actually go check on them. You'll also need water and electricity, so make sure that you have lines going out to that.

The area should be level with the most sun exposure, or at least six hours a day. You should try to orient it, and if you don't have the ability to do so, you should get some growing lights.

Ideally, you should try to avoid putting a greenhouse near trees that cast shadows, since this happens a lot during the winter. Ideally, put it near some deciduous trees.

You should make sure that you also have enough drainage. Put some landscape cloth under the area, and add some gravel to this, in order to help create a god surface, but with drainage and won't make the weeds grow.

If you do have issues with this, you should contact a landscaper to help you choose the location. The right place will allow for the plants to grow, and in turn, it will help it become the greenhouse garden you desire.

This chapter discussed what you need before you begin. Knowing this will help you choose the site in a fitting manner, making it easier for you to grow whatever you want.

Chapter 2: Factors that Affect Greenhouse Gardening

There are a few particular factors that can affect the ability of plants to grow in a greenhouse, and it's important to understand what each of them are. This chapter will give you these factors, and what the best way to control them is.

Water

Water is an obvious one, but often, the biggest problem isn't water period, but having too much water. You need to be mindful of this, and ideally, check to make sure that you do give it enough, and not overwater it. You probably will have to water it at least once a day, but you should definitely check it.

Sometimes, you can stick your finger into the soil in order to check it. If it's wet, don't bother. You should make sure that the soil and pots have good drainage so that it can leave. If you don't, there is a chance that you might end up killing the plant. Some can be watered any other day, but do check each of them before you begin so that you're not overwatering any of them.

Light

Light is another factor to consider. You should try for full sun for everything, and make sure to cut down anything too excess if needed. You can always put more shade in if needed, but you definitely need to watch.

You should also make sure that you give your plants as much light as you can. Remember, you can reduce the sun exposure, but it's often hard to bring more light in, short of artificial light.

During the winter, you might need artificial lamps, so make sure that you do look into this, and make sure not to skimp on this step.

Ventilation

You might not think ventilation matters when it comes to plants but it's a huge thing, and often, it's actually one of the key factors in helping to regulate a greenhouse. Without proper ventilation, the temperature, air, and even how many pests breed or don't breed do get affected by this, and if you have good ventilation, the plants will pollinate.

You will feel the air if it's not fully ventilated. There are often more pests, mold and mildew, and even fungi and other diseases that will wreak havoc on the plants, and it's often quite a troublesome thing to deal with. This is a simple fix though, and something you can change with just adding in a fan, or even some windows. Sometimes, even just having rooftop vents allow this to leave in a natural sense. A fan, or any means to circulate the air, along with a screen and such, can help control the entire environment, allowing for a much fresher atmosphere. Think about it, would you want to be stuck in a small house without fresh air? Probably not, so take the time and install proper ventilation in your greenhouse before you put the plants in.

Humidity

And finally there is humidity. Humidity is a huge part in plant growth, and while some plants can handle very humid climes, it's actually not the best thing for plants that are grown in a greenhouse, since it can actually make it harder to grow. They should be around 70 percent, to up to 85 percent when growing, and you shouldn't have it above 90 percent if you possibly can handle it. Why is humidity bad though? Well, too much of it is actually a bad thing, since it makes plants weaker, but not only that, it actually can cause fungal diseases to form, and bolting as well, and it can cause plants that are otherwise healthy to limp, and other problems that will only get worse, and it's definitely not fun to deal with.

if you do have to worry about humidity, there are simple solutions, including venting, as said before, exhausting the air, and also limiting the water. You should increase the humidity by adding water to the floor of the greenhouse, since it will help with the humidity levels. You can do that, or even just put water containers on the floor to help it evaporate to the levels that you want it to be at.

When it comes to greenhouse gardening, these environmental factors totally matter, and it's very imporntat that you know how to prevent these whenever you can. These are the ones to watch out for, and in turn, once you do pay attention to this, you'll be able to have healthier plants, and better gardening as a result of this as well.

Chapter 3: How to Control the Environment

So how do you control the environment fully? What are some of the key things to have in a greenhouse before you begin? Well, let's discuss that. This chapter will talk about how you can control a greenhouse environment in order to make sure that nothing gets thrown off, and the plants are left healthy, and happy as well.

First thing's first, consider a heating and cooling system. While heating might not be needed during the day, since it does get cold at night, it can make things a lot harder for the plants in terms of growth, and that in turn can definitely be a problem. With heating, you have a few options.

You can get one of those electric heaters to circulate the air in there and to heat it up. Small heaters that are oil or gas are also good alternatives. You can also install solar heaters that are made for greenhouses if you want to go fully green. For the plants in general, have some heat lamps and heating cables if needed too, since this will help with making sure that the plants are nice and toasty. In any case, you want to make sure that the greenhouse is vented so that you're not letting the air stagnate, and also that these heaters have a means to shut off automatically. For cooling systems, take some water barrels, or even buckets, and this can be used to help keep plants warm, but also cool when the sun goes away.

Shading is another important thing. Sometimes, your plants might get too much light. In that case, making sure that you reduce the sunlight that they're getting is imperative. Getting those shade cloths that you can put over stuff is quite helpful, but also those rolling screens can help, and even some plastic shading can be used to help control this. If you think the plants are getting too much, you should inspect them to see if there are signs of burning or drying out. If so, you want to make sure that you cover them as needed.

With ventilation, get those vents or a fan that will be able to open and close. There are some super cheap ones that will help naturally move air, or you can get the hydraulic ones that will open and close automatically.

Gutters are also a huge plus when it comes to getting some natural water, or even to help with the rain barrels thing. You can use this to collect it, and if you have anything along the greenhouse, you can simply prevent these plans from getting too much water.

When it comes to gravel for the floor, get the pea gravel. Putting this on top of landscape fabric will help to keep the place from being overgrown with weeds, but there is another reason for this. If you do put this there, and water them, it will naturally keep the greenhouse at a cooler temperature.

Finally, there are pests. Particularly, aunts, gnats, ladybugs, and spiders. The best way to prevent them is to take the necessary precautions. If you see ants, start to consider perimeter treatment. If you start to see gnats, you need to make sure that you're not overwatering the plants, since this is often the reason why they show up.

If you do see some eggs on the plants, or even larva, you should take a look at them, and I they're beneficial for the place, let them sit around.

You should also remember that not every buy is a bad bug. For example, ladybugs and green lacewings actually help the garden. Spiders will also kill bugs, and you should consider getting the predators into there to help protect the plants. You should make sure to not have whiteflies though, since those are bad for the garden, and they're actually very hard to remove from there, so make sure you begin to learn the difference, and do take your time to establish the pests.

All in all, you should check the plants before bringing them in, and after you do to ensure that none of them are harmful for the greenhouse, but instead are beneficial for the environment.

This chapter discussed some of the environmental factors to watch out for, and why it matters that you take some time and look at the state of the greenhouse before you go any further.

Chapter 4: The Best Plants to Grow in a Greenhouse

So what are the best plants to grow in a greenhouse you'll be surprised, because there are a few that definitely do the job and then some. This chapter will go over the best types of plants to grow, why that is, and what you should consider when you're trying to grow them.

Onions and Shallots

This is a great one to start with during the fall, since they are super low-maintenance. That's right, these actually don't really need much upkeep, despite not being ready until the summer after. However, you will definitely still want to make sure that they get transplanted into the ground during the spring.

You should consider the reliable red onions, shallots, and some yellow onions in many cases, as these tend to have the best growing life out of everything.

Leafy Greens

These are another super popular vegetable to start with. It's basically anything that normally belongs in a salad.

So why are these good? Well, they grow in virtually the same way regardless of it being in the ground or in a potter. You also don't need to even really do much for it, and other than knowing basic stuff, it definitely is pretty simple. They're also pretty, come in many different tastes and remarkable colors, and you can use this in virtually anything, from soups, to salads, to even various side dishes as well. If you want to sell them as well, these make a decent income as well.

Spinach

Kind of in the same vein as leafy greens, spinach is one of the most popular and best greenhouse plants for you to grow. It is something you can cut directly from the garden in order to use it. It's very healthy, with a whole bonanza of various vitamins and minerals that you can get instantly from this. It's also super simple to grow, so you won't have issues when growing this, and it's considered one of the best, and one of the easiest plants to grow in a greenhouse garden.

Garlic

Garlic is another super simplest, since it has a lot of different varieties that you can choose from, and it is a good one to plant during the fall. They're similar in nature to growing onions, in that they do have a long season of growing, and often won't be ready to be used until the summer after, but it's worth it. garlic is one of the main ingredients of various cuisine out there, and you can get a whole lot of vitamins and minerals from it. It's also a very powerful antibacterial as well, and it's full of yummy flavor. There are many different varieties to choose from, and you can grow this directly in the garden for the best results.

Broad beans

Broad beans are another great one to grow in a greenhouse since you can start them early, and actually harvest them during the spring as well, and can be harvested a month earlier than most other plants that are sown during the spring. It's super quick to begin, and you can also get the kinds that are quick to be established during the autumn, so you'll be able to have a lot of these immediately. Typically, if you get them a bit wilted, it'll be a whole lot better.

Cucumbers

Cucumbers are a great one to incorporate into salads, since you've probably had this a lot since you were a kid. They're good raw, or even just with some salads and other dishes. They're definitely a great one to have, and are good for greenhouse gardening, since they do need a controlled atmosphere for best results. Sometimes, people will shrink wrap them to help keep the purity once you've finished harvesting to keep them around for way longer.

Asparagus

If you've got a lot of space, one other vegetable to consider is asparagus. These are great to put in a greenhouse, and starting them during the fall will definitely yield results. While they often take a bit of time to grow, they do offer a lot once they're established, and you can get up to 25 spears of asparagus per crop, and it will continue for at least 25 years, which is a super long time. You can begin them in the fall in a greenhouse, transplant them, and get them established, but it's important to note that they take a little bit of time.

Winter Salads and Carrots

Winter salads are often a great one to consider for a greenhouse. These are essentially tasty leafy greens that you can cut in the greenhouse, and it will continue to grow. Lambs lettuce, mustard, and land cress are the three main types that allow you to have a little bit of extra to your salads, and it can even bring forth a peppery flavor too, giving you a nice little spicy extra to all your favorite salads.

Finally, there are carrots, and these are great to have, since you can sow these in November within a greenhouse, or if you do it outside, as late as July. They can grow all during the winter, and carrots are used in so many different things, that they're worth the effort.

Chapter 5: Greenhouse Gardening Tips

Now that you know the basics of greenhouse gardening, let's discuss a few tips to help you get the most out of this. This chapter will dive into a few helpful tips to make your greenhouse the best that it can be.

First, use the greenhouse for seasonal plants, in order to begin them so that they're fruitful during the peak growing season. If you do this, you'll be able to get a leg up when it's time to put them outside. Ideally, you should plant these during the winter, use heat sources when it starts to get cooler, and also consider a propagation mat. This is a way to easily heat seeds up in order to encourage growth especially if you're looking to save money.

If you don't want to spend a ton of money on light sources, get those small fluorescent strips that you can hang right above the plants. This is a simple, and cheap way to grow stuff fast.

When using fertilizer, work to dilute them. If you use too much, you will start to burn the roots.

You should consider investing in a wireless transmitter to look at the highs and lows of the greenhouse. This is a good way to make sure it doesn't go below the threshold, and if you do use this, consider having it notify you whenever the temperature goes below what it should ideally be.

When watering, you want to water them from the bottom up to prevent it from getting to damp in the pot. You should also, during the winter months or when it's cold, use warm water to water plants. Cold water is actually a way to stop growth, since it'll send the seeds into shock.

If the plant already looks sickly, don't overwinter it. It actually will spread the pests and blight to each of the other pests.

If you're looking for a way to help with germination, get those propagation mats. It will help it grow and you won't have to worry on heat as much.

One way to make sure everything is growing okay, is to get a greenhouse journal. This can be a small task you take on that will record the temperatures of the journal and a daily summary. You can include what was planted, and how it was planted, and how long it's been since they have been, and if anything has germinated. This is a great way to help you keep track of whether or not a plant is growing, and it can help you make sure that you're doing the right thing for each of these plants.

Growing a greenhouse garden is a ton of fun, but It's often quite hard at the beginning. But, if you make sure that you do this right, and you do take the time to learn how to adequately grow a greenhouse garden, you'll be able to nab the benefits, and have fun as well.

Growing greenhouse vegetables is a great way to help get some nutritious foods into your body, allowing for better, more remunerative growing in your greenhouse garden. With that being said, you should take some time, look over each of the veggies, and find the one that best fits you. Sometimes, it might take a bit to find the perfect plants to grow, but once you do, it's a fun adventure that you will definitely enjoy.

Conclusion

Now that you have all the information that you want to obtain, it's time for you to go out, and create your own greenhouse garden. Greenhouse gardens are quite fun to create, and they have a lead of amazing benefits that you can net from this. With greenhouse gardens, you'll be able to grow plants all year round, and make sure that you have some amazing crops when the growing season starts.

It does take a bit of time to begin this, but once you do, you'll be well on your way. With that being said, your next step is really pretty simple. You should start to consider the different types of plants to grow in there, and also the ideal greenhouse for yourself. Even if it's a small greenhouse, it's a great way to help you have the best, and healthiest garden that you can have. It's the beginning of a new adventure for you, and as long as you do this with a smile on your face, it will definitely be fun.

BONUS BOOK SAMPLE:

Medicinal Plants: The Complete And Perfect Guide Reference To The Top 8 Medicinal Plants That Can Be Grown In Your Backyard That Cure Ailments!

Copyright 2018

Disclaimer

This book is not intended as a substitute for the medical advice of physicians. The reader should regularly consult a physician in matters relating to his/her health and particularly with respect to any symptoms that may require diagnosis or medical attention.

Although the author and publisher have made every effort to ensure that the information in this book was correct at press time, the author and publisher do not assume and hereby disclaim any liability to any party for any loss, damage, or disruption caused by errors or omissions, whether such errors or omissions result from negligence, accident, or any other cause.

This document is geared towards providing exact and reliable information in regards to the topic and issue covered. The publication is sold with the idea that the publisher is not required to render accounting, officially permitted, or otherwise, qualified services. If advice is necessary, legal or professional, a practiced individual in the profession should be ordered.

- From a Declaration of Principles which was accepted and approved equally by a Committee of the American Bar Association and a Committee of Publishers and Associations.

In no way is it legal to reproduce, duplicate, or transmit any part of this document in either electronic means or in printed format. Recording of this publication is strictly prohibited and any storage of this document is not allowed unless with written permission from the publisher. All rights reserved.

The information provided herein is stated to be truthful and consistent, in that any liability, in terms of inattention or otherwise, by any usage or abuse of any policies, processes, or directions contained within is the solitary and utter responsibility of the recipient reader. Under no circumstances will any legal responsibility or blame be held against the publisher for any reparation, damages, or monetary loss due to the information herein, either directly or indirectly.

Respective authors own all copyrights not held by the publisher.

The information herein is offered for informational purposes solely, and is universal as so. The presentation of the information is without contract or any type of guarantee assurance.

The trademarks that are used are without any consent, and the publication of the trademark is without permission or backing by the trademark owner. All trademarks and brands within this book are for clarifying purposes only and are the owned by the owners themselves, not affiliated with this document.

Introduction

Do you like medicinal plants and herbs? Lots of times, medicinal plants are a way to help take care of the body and better it, and are a great alternative to typical medicine.

But, what are the best ones out there?

There are many different types of medicinal plants for you to choose from, and some of them can actually be grown right in your backyard. It's super nifty, and very convenient. The array of plants that you can choose from is vast, and it can be a bit overwhelming at first.

This book will go over what you need to know about medicinal plants, including the top eight ones that will help you in life, and how to grow them in your backyard. By the end of this, you'll be able to grow a variety of different medicinal plants, all of which can be used to help better your body, and make it stronger as a result of these actions. If you've ever wanted to better your life, medicinal plants are the way to go, and there are so many that you can try, but these eight ones will allow you to get the most that you can from it, and also the myriad of health benefits as well.

I used to wonder a bit about how medicinal plants can change my life. I learned from this, that there are many different benefits to them, and as I continued to cultivate, I learned more and more. I wrote this book so that you can get the benefits of these medicinal herbs right away, so that you too can have a better, healthier life.

Chapter 1: Garlic

When you think of garlic, you probably think of vampires, or the fact that your breath will smell. However, this plant is so much more than that. It's a very common spice used in cooking, and almost every single recipe calls for it. But, what's so great about garlic, and why is it considered one of the top eight medicinal plants out there? Well, you're about to find out.

The first thing, is that garlic is super easy to cultivate. That means that if you plant it in your backyard, typically in a shade or partial sun area, you'll net a lot of this. It's a great one that you can use I a variety of dishes. It's a super powerful flavor, so I don't suggest eating it raw, unless you're into the taste of that.

But, that's not all. It can heal a lot of different diseases that are out there. It's actually a very powerful antibacterial and antiviral, and it can be used to help naturally boost the immune system as well, so you don't have to do a whole lot, but have the garlic that you want to have. With garlic, its super simple to add as well, in that you literally just have to put it into a dish to truly get the benefits of it.

It's also super low-calorie, like a lot of the other popular medicinal plants out there, and it can be used to get a ton of nutrients. What it lacks in calories, it has in nutrients, including Vitamin B6, C, Fiber, and even Manganese, which are all very popular elements that can be used to help keep the body in top shape.

It has a very pungent smell to it, as you'll begin to notice. That's because it's got Sulphur in it, and that actually is a way to help naturally keep away predators, so you don't have to worry about other insects or animals trying to eat this, because it's way too pungent for those guys.

Now, what does it protect? Well, if you are at risk for cancer, you can use garlic to help protect yourself against this.

It also will help the digestive system, in that it will aid you in absorbing nutrients, and also help with any excess grime that's left in the body. It also can be used to help reduce blood pressure and other cardiovascular issues as well, which is good, since that's the number one killer. It also can prevent allergies and improve your iron levels and metabolism of these elements. Finally, if you've got a toothache, you can take this, and it actually can be used to help better it, and that can help if you're getting some work done.

It's a means to help naturally detoxify the body, which is actually really good. With garlic, it might taste a bit too pungent for some, but even if you just cook it for fragrance more than anything, you'll be able to net the benefits of this right away. It's a great medicinal plant that has such a wide variety of uses, and it's one herb and plant that can markedly change your overall life, and your viewpoint on all of the different types of plants that you can cultivate.

Chapter 2: Spinach

Another great plant that you can have in your arsenal is spinach. It's an edible plant that's native to Central Asian areas. It's great for salads and other vegetables, but it's also good for the body as well. Spinach actually has a lot of great vitamins to it, and it's got a lot of powerful vitamins and minerals. Spinach does have a lot of great vitamins in it as well, including Vitamins A, K, C, B1, and other minerals including folate, magnesium, iron, selenium, zinc, and phosphorus. Not only that, spinach does taste great, and whether you like it raw or cooked doesn't really matter. There are lots of great benefits that you can get from spinach if you include it in your diet.

For starters, it isn't just the minerals and vitamins listed above, but it's also riboflavin, luetine, and beta carotene that are also in there. They do improve your heart health, and the nervous system, and it can be used to help prevent heart disease, and other nervous system issues.

It's also really good for your eyesight, in that the vitamins that are in it, including Vitamin A, can be used to help keep your eye health at the top shape it can be. It also can be used to naturally make your bones stronger, allowing you to prevent various diseases and the like when it comes to this.

Cancer can also be protected from this as well, and you'll be able to fight this as well if you do have some spinach, since it has a lot of antioxidants in it.

Speaking of antioxidants, you can actually reduce the chances of having DNA damages, and that means that you can stop aging, and even cancer if you have this in your diet. It can eliminate the free radicals in the body, allowing for a better, more rewarding result from all of this.

With that in mind, it can also help to reduce the levels of blood pressure, preventing insomnia, obesity, neuritis, and even tumors, and it's a great solution for not just those that want to lose weight, but it also can be use for those that have diabetes, and even cancer.

It can also be used to help with cholesterol, especially if it's getting too high. Sometimes, if you balance this out, you can prevent a whole lot of bad things from happening in the body.

Finally, with the amount of Vitamin K in it, you can actually prevent nervous system issues with this, and in turn, it will allow you to live longer, protect yourself against degenerative mental conditions, and overall, you'll feel way healthier as well.

With spinach, you'll be able to effectively take it, and actually be able to use it with a variety of foods. With the number of different vitamins and minerals in it, you'll be able to have a much better, more rewarding life, and you'll be able to protect yourself against many of the degenerative conditions that are out there, and in turn be able to live a longer, more healthy life.

Chapter 3: Chamomile

Have you ever had chamomile tea? It's a really nice, calming tea that can be used to relax the way the body feels, and overall, feel better and sleepier. But, did you know that chamomile is actually a medicinal plant that can help you with many conditions in the body? That's right, it's not just a tea that can be used to relax you, it's actually a very powerful plant that can be used to help kickstart the digestive tract, and make it better for you.

The way you extract it, is via the flower heads. Lots of times, it's used in the form of the tea, but sometimes, you can use dried chamomile in cooking, and typically the ointments that are made are using the heads of said flower.

The main thing that chamomile does, is that it can help with the gas in your body, and also reduce the instance of nausea, the need to vomit, and even the buildup of bile that's located in the digestive tract, so if you're feeling sick, sometimes having this can be the surefire way to make yourself feel better. It works for general sickness, morning sickness, and the like as well.

It's also a natural astringent, which means that it will tighten the blood vessels and the tissues that are in there. What does this mean for you? Well, it can be topically applied to wounds in order to help stop the bleeding, and it can be used to naturally heal. If you're stressed, it can be used to help reduce the blood pressure levels, and it will make you feel way better as well.

However, along with that, it can be used to effectively and without fail help to reduce the bleeding and the presence of the wound, thereby healing them. If you do get bit by something poisonous, you can rub chamomile on this wound, and it does help.

Both versions of this, including roman and German chamomile, can be used to help reduce the levels of swelling in the body, and that can be used if you do get a bug bite or a sting that does tend to fester a nasty bite as a result of this. If you're allergic to bee stings, or if you get a nasty one, rubbing some chamomile on this can make a huge difference in the presence of this wound.

It also can be used for hemorrhoids since it will reduce the levels of swelling and stinging feelings in that area as well.

So yes you can use chamomile for more than just teas. It has a wide variety of uses, and a lot that can be done with it, and this chapter showcased what's so great about it, and why you should consider chamomile as a backyard plant.

Chapter 4: Echinacea

Another great medicinal plant, and probably one of the best for almost any condition, is echinacea. This is a plant with really tall stems, and it's got flowers that are typically pink and purple, so if you do plant it in the garden, it will actually make a very pretty addition to it, since the colors are bright. There are nine different types, but only three are actually considered medicinal ones, and they are purpurea, angustifolia, and pallida. These three are the ones you should be looking for if you're gong to use this medicinal plant.

Now, echinacea is actually one of the best plants to kickstart the immune system, if you're trying to fight off a cold. It will naturally boost it, and you can add this as a spice or an addition as a green to the foods that you eat, and it will drive the body's immune system to high levels. It's definitely a great one to have if you're starting to get sick, fighting off a cold or a flu, or have a viral and bacterial infection that you're struggling to get rid of.

This is also a plant that can be used in its entirety for medicinal purposes, since it has all of the properties in each part. It does work with the chemicals currently in the body in order to fight off various fungi that might be there, inflammation that might come about, and even help with fighting the flu.

So how good is this for inflammation reduction? Well, it can be used to help with the stiffness of joints, making arthritic conditions much easier to cope with. It does naturally help with inflammation that's present in the body as well, and it definitely can help with reducing free radicals or even autoimmune diseases that might be there.

But, the core reason you'd use this plant is for prevention and protection against various conditions and instances. It actually can markedly reduce the chances of a cold, or even bronchitis, sore throats, and coughing too. It is really nice, and once you get the health benefits there, it will make all the difference. The roots are used in many different forms, and you can get the most health benefits from there, if you're looking for the best location on the plant to get this sort of thing.

It's a great addition to your garden, and it actually can look good, but also help people out as well. It's one that is recommended if you're looking to truly make your garden look awesome, but also a means to help if you're looking to fight off various conditions and the like that might be around. It can change your life, and it can change the way your body and mind feel as soon as you take this.

Chapter 5: Thyme

Thyme is a super popular cooking spice, and lots of people tend to use it in a variety of recipes. It's also a very nice-smelling plant, and it works well and does the job and then some. It's pretty as well, and can be a nice green addition to the garden if that's what you're looking for.

As for what it can do in terms of medicinally, typically, the oil of this plant, the flowers, and the leaves are what are used to net many of the different health benefits. This is also a plant that's been around for a super long time, dating back thousands of years ago in ancient Egypt. It was a very popular plant to use when it came to embalming mummies, and also for healing many of the medical conditions. It's an old, but also very popular plant, and it has a wide variety of different uses.

Typically, thyme is anti-fungal, antiviral and also antiseptic and parasitic, meaning that it can naturally heal the body all over, and it can even prevent various conditions that might be around.

It can be used to help prevent colds if you feel like one of them is coming on, since it can be used to naturally boost the immune system up and then some. If you know of bacterial infections in food, such as maybe a recent food outbreak that you might worry about, using this can help to protect the body from this, and in turn, protect it from food poisoning as well, so it's a good way to fortify the body and make it strong.

If you have high blood pressure, you can naturally use this to help balance it out and reduce the levels of it, thereby controlling it better, and reduce the chances for heart conditions and the like.

It also will reduce the instances of colon cancer too, so if you're worried about that, you should definitely use this.

If you have skin issues, such as red skin, skin dryness, swelling, and other issues, you can rub this onto the skin, and it will help to reduce the instance of it, and even work to get rid of the condition. This in turn will make your skin much healthier, make you look younger, and you'll feel way better as well.

If you have a cough or a cold, having this will help to reduce the instance of it, and in turn, it will make the cold and cough so much easier on your body as well. It's one that you can have right when the flu season begins too in order to help prepare the body.

Finally, it relaxes you, and it will calm the nervous system down and make you feel better. It is a good one to take before bed, since it can help with sleep, and if you're feeling anxious about something, you can use thyme in order to help with those instances, and it in turn can give you a much more restful sleep as a result of this.

With all of these factors, thyme is definitely considered one of the best medicinal plants if you're thinking about trying to have overall body health and wellness. It works to better you, to make your life easier, and it's actually super easy to grow. Just one of those plants can net you a large amount of this, and with the fact that there are so many uses for this, and so much you can do with it, you'll be able to definitely have a much better result from this, and in turn, help to fortify your body to protect it against everything that could possibly be there, and whatever might go wrong.

Chapter 6: Catnip

Did you know that catnip isn't just something for cats? While it is hilarious to give this to your cat, just to see how they might react, there is a lot more that you can do with this in fact. You can use this in many different ways to help yourself as a human, and it's considered one of the best medicinal plants out there. Why is that? Why do people turn to catnip to help themselves? Well, you're about to find out. This chapter will talk about why catnip is a great medicinal plant, and just what it can do to help better your body.

So what is catnip? Well, it's actually not just called catnip, it's also called catmint, and it's actually a native plant to central Asia and Europe, and it actually can be cultivated right in your backyard. You can go to the nursery to get this, and it has a lot of amazing health benefits to it. just because it sounds like it's meant for cats doesn't mean it is just meant for cats. In fact, humans get a lot of amazing benefits from this.

The first thing, is that it can be used to help you with any problems that you might have mentally. Think about it, catnip is so great for cats and attractive to them, since it does give them a "high" in a sense, and it can be used to sedate them, and in humans, it does the same thing, in a much more controlled manner. It can be used to help reduce stress, since it can help with chronic anxiety. If you consume it, you'll start to realize that you're less stressed too, and it can be used to help strengthen the immune system.

With that in mind, it also can help with insomnia and restlessness. It actually has been used for thousands of years, and due to the sedative way that it is made, it can actually slow everything down, giving you a relaxed and calm state. You'll be able to sleep better if you take this, and it will be both more restful, and also less disturbed. Catnip tea is actually something great that you can have right before bed to give you the most refreshing sleep.

If you have digestive issues, such as constipation, gas, bloating, and cramping, it actually can be rectified with catnip. It's super relaxing, and I can help to reduce inflammation in the body, since the organic compounds in this can actually help reduce the inflammation and the knots in the digestive system, and this in turn will help with discomfort and tightness. It also can be used to help with reducing nausea.

It also is a great way to get toxins out of the body. It can be used to help with inflammation from said toxins, making you feel way better, and also have much better healing as well. If your body has a lot of toxic elements to it, this is a way to get rid of them and to eliminate them.

It's also one of the best ways to naturally reduce a migraine or a headache, and it's arguably one of the best natural means too.

Finally, it can help with a toothache, simply by relaxing the body. If you're getting dental work done, have some catnip after that to help with the tooth issues, since it will also de-stress the body and lower all of the pressure on it, making it easier for you to relax.

Catnip isn't just for cats, but rather, it's a great way to help a human feel better, and also to help get many of the same benefits. Just drinking this as a tea can change your life, and it's considered one of the best medicinal plants for anything related to tensions, tension headaches, and the like.

Chapter 7: Marigold

This is another pretty flower that actually has a wide array of health benefits. Marigold is a very pretty reddish-gold flower that can be used in a lot of different types of soils that are out there. They are colorful, and can be used to help add a little bit of extra color to your garden. But, it's also a medicinal plant, and using this can actually help with many problems, even scar reduction and curing skin conditions as well. It's a great anti-inflammatory plant that can be used topically to help with allergies and rashes, and it does the job fast and well.

Basically, if you have any sort of skin condition, whether it be a wound, a wart, bite, acne, ulcers, or even rashes and sunburns, you want to use this topically on the area. This is a great ointment to help with this, since it can make a huge difference in the overall nature of this. It actually can be used to reduce the instance of this, but it also can heal the wound too, as in the case of a cut or bruise, and if your skin is dry and blistered, it can help rejuvenate the area, making it better for you as a result. It's a very powerful skin antioxidant, and it does the job well.

If you use this as a tea, it actually can do wonders for the digestive system. This can help with lowering the symptoms of bowel disease, such as colitis, allowing you to have a better digestive tract. It also can be used to treat acid reflux, gastritis, and even stomach ulcers. It can also reduce the instance of both stomach and menstrual cramps, which will help with soothing it as a result.

Having this in the form of drops creates a powerful immune system booster, and in turn, it can be used to help with the symptoms of coughs, fevers, sore throats, and also helping to promote general immune system health. It's not just a pretty plant, but it's a powerful plant as well.

It's also the best solution to toothaches and the like, so if you get a lot of those, you should consider having a little bit of marigold in your home. It can directly fight the bacteria and reduce the tension in the area, and when it's taken as a tea, it can do a lot.

With a lot of the bacteria, sometimes you need something strong, and marigold can do the job and then some when it comes to this. definitely do consider this one, since it can look great in the garden, but also fight off many of these conditions as well without having too many issues.

Chapter 8: Sage

Finally we have sage which is a great plant and herb. It's got really nice flowers, which in turn can help bring life to your garden, but also leaves that are very soft, and they look nice as well. This is one of the best home garden plants for a variety of reasons. It's simple to cultivate, can help cure many conditions, and it's got a ton of antioxidants and nutrients within it. But what's so great about sage? Why consider this for your garden? Well, you're about to find out.

It's actually one of the best plants to help with memory and cognition, boating both of these things. The best part, is that you don't even need to worry about how much you have to take, it actually can be beneficial even in the smallest amounts, and it can help with recalling stuff and retaining information in many people. It allows for better concentration on topics, which means that if you take this while in school or before a hard example, it can make a huge difference. It might seem subtle, but it can effectively boost the brain levels and overall wellness and happiness.

Then there is inflammation, which was mentioned before. Sage leaves can be chewed on if you don't want to use it as a spice. However, this might be like garlic, which isn't very pleasant due to the taste of it, but it actually allows for direct absorption of the compounds directly into the system. You can also steep the leaves to get the same thing, but if you have inflammation, you can use this to help reduce it. It's very anti-inflammatory, and it extends to health areas such as the realm of gout and arthritis, and it can help with general inflammation of any system, including cardiovascular. Inflammation there tends to cause heart disease and blood pressure, and by simply having sage, it can improve the effects of this, allowing you to have many different benefits from this.

It also can instantly reduce some of the other conditions that might be present in the body. Since it does work as a natural memory booster, it can also be used for overall emotions and wellness. It can instantly reduce the instances of depression, and the effects of it. By having this, you'll start to feel better as well.

When you use it topically on an area, it can help to heal wounds that might be there, since it is a powerful antibacterial and an antiviral. It also can help with toothache if you suffer from that, and it can also prevent infections in both the throat, lungs, and even the nose. It's arguably one of the best herbs to be used as an antiseptic.

Finally, it's a powerful antioxidant, in that it can be used to help with chronic conditions and those degenerative diseases that can debilitate and create dangerous health problems later on down the road, such as cancers and the like. The cause of many of these, including cancer, is by free radicals, which are the products of cell metabolism that tend to attack those cells that are healthy, which mutates them. However, sage can actually prevent these from creating that stress, neutralizing the free radicals and helping the body out.

Simply put, sage is great for this, and it can do so much for the body as well. with that being said, it's a great addition to the garden, and it's a medicinal plant you can grow in your backyard.

Conclusion

Medical plants are some of the best plants to have in your home, because not only are they great for the garden, and they are healthy for you as well. They also can many times give a nice bit of life to any garden, since they do tend to be pretty as well. medicinal plants can get the job done, and they do it well, and you'll be able to avail yourself of the many benefits that many have gotten from it.

With that being said, it's important that you focus on the next step. The next one is simple, and that is to start getting some of these plants. The best way to do it is by going to your local organic nursery, and finding out which ones they have. Typically, all of these are available in some way, shape or form. You plant them according to the instructions, and then, you can watch it grow. Medicinal plants are there to help you out, to make your life easier, and you'll be able to use them right from the comfort of your backyard without any sorts of problems.